T0067197

How to Raise Your Children with
Wisdom and Awareness

A CHANNELED BOOK BY

LYNN BARIBAULT

BALBOA.
PRESS
A DIVISION OF HAY HOUSE

Copyright © 2017 Lynn Baribault.
Author Photo by Pat LaChance

All rights reserved. No part of this book may be used or reproduced by any means, graphic, electronic, or mechanical, including photocopying, recording, taping or by any information storage retrieval system without the written permission of the author except in the case of brief quotations embodied in critical articles and reviews.

This book is a work of non-fiction. Unless otherwise noted, the author and the publisher make no explicit guarantees as to the accuracy of the information contained in this book and in some cases, names of people and places have been altered to protect their privacy.

Balboa Press books may be ordered through booksellers or by contacting:

Balboa Press
A Division of Hay House
1663 Liberty Drive
Bloomington, IN 47403
www.balboapress.com
1 (877) 407-4847

Because of the dynamic nature of the Internet, any web addresses or links contained in this book may have changed since publication and may no longer be valid. The views expressed in this work are solely those of the author and do not necessarily reflect the views of the publisher, and the publisher hereby disclaims any responsibility for them.

The author of this book does not dispense medical advice or prescribe the use of any technique as a form of treatment for physical, emotional, or medical problems without the advice of a physician, either directly or indirectly. The intent of the author is only to offer information of a general nature to help you in your quest for emotional and spiritual well-being. In the event you use any of the information in this book for yourself, which is your constitutional right, the author and the publisher assume no responsibility for your actions.

Any people depicted in stock imagery provided by Thinkstock are models, and such images are being used for illustrative purposes only.
Certain stock imagery © Thinkstock.

Print information available on the last page.

ISBN: 978-1-5043-8373-8 (sc)
ISBN: 978-1-5043-8374-5 (e)

Library of Congress Control Number: 2017910373

Balboa Press rev. date: 07/24/2017

Dedications:

To my daughters, Kimmaly and Manichanh who are the main thread of my life. Je suis fière de vous et je vous aime de tout mon coeur.

To my grandmother, Clémence, my sister, my friend of olde.

To the Spirit of *Grandmother who through her wisdom and encouragements spearheaded this book by gathering amazing Spirits for me to channel.

To my mother, Hélène who opened the doors to alternative healing modalities.

* Lori Wilson's Spirit Guide. An Ancient Shoshone Elder. From hereon, if I say "Grandmother", this is who I am referring to.

Acknowledgments

A special thank you to my co-conspirators and incredible supporters, Richard and Suzanne. Merci.

To my family, especially my cousin, Martine and my aunt Suzette who wholeheartedly trusted me at difficult moments in their lives. You allowed me to grow and gain confidence in myself. A special thank you to my cousin Patrick for his time and patience in taking beautiful photographs of me. Merci.

To my friend Sharon Vettoretto of Intuitively Yours Healing Arts for her friendship and her creative talent in painting my vision for the book cover. You are amazing!

I am very grateful to my great friends Karen and John for their constant presence in my life.

To Kimberly, Dave, Melanie and Nathalie who have always believed that I would actually finish this book and who can now tell me: "We told you so".

As well, un grand merci to my amazing friend Sylvie for always adding zest to my life. Your laughter and love of life are contagious.

I am also very grateful to Lori Wilson for her guidance in editing parts of this book and for allowing me to share Grandmother's wisdom. Thank you.

A book is born from a message....

A few years ago, I was told by a Spirit Guide *Grandmother, as channeled by an intuitive teacher here in Guelph named Lori Wilson, founder of Inner Access 101, that I was to write a book. Being a very linear thinker at times, I was surprised and quickly discredited the notion that I would ever achieve this as I could not believe that people would actually want to read what I wrote. A few years later, I decided it was time to take another course with Lori. The course was called Access Intuition 101 where one learns how to get in touch with eight unique sources of invisible wisdom available in the universe. During this course, I was truly amazed at how many kinds of Guides one could have access to, from Spirits, Shamans and Elders, and, even incredibly, to animals and insects in nature. It was an eye opener to say the least.

Lori is a very calm person who has great confidence that we all have skills which allow us to maximize our own intuition that all of us have. Wouldn't it be a great world if we could all be such positive influences in each other's lives? Life, with daily kindness and caring, would be a wonder to live in. During one of the days' activities, Lori's Spirit Guide she channels, and whom she lovingly calls Grandmother, told me once again that I would be writing a book. I asked Lori to ask Grandmother what exactly I was supposed to write about as, again, I was totally baffled. The message given to me was to write about how one lives life when given day-to-day principles to live by. This was not to be a scientific book or even an "all revelations" book, but a book about good, old, simple common sense and how regular people can live better lives if they follow the said principles. Grandmother elaborated that this was to specifically be a book for parents, which rang true for me as I have at times, being a teacher, helped parents parent their children.

As you know, being a parent does not come with a recipe book. Even though we try our best, children sometimes stump us because of who they are, and how they react to situations. We are all individuals and we cannot assume that because we, as parents, are a certain way, our children will react in the same fashion. As well, our children are often much better at certain aspects of life than we are. Hence, we have to be open to the fact that even though we are the adults, we can still learn from someone younger than us. This is a wonder and a difficulty all at once, as we, as parents, need to take stock of who we are, and be able to change, accepting guidance in whichever form it comes.

So, as I have been told many times by now that I was to write a book and, even though I am still unsure of what and who would read the book, I have decided to trust the very wise Grandmother and start the process of writing, hence putting ink on paper. Let us see how this unfolds and what ideas come forth as I quiet down and listen carefully to the world just beyond, where amazing Guides reside. Guides who are always ready to impart us with incredible knowledge and, as I write this, I feel them surrounding me, cool energies lingering close by, therefore, here and now we begin.

* Lori Wilson's Spirit Guide. An ancient Shoshone Elder. From hereon, if I say "Grandmother", this is who I am referring to.

April 14, 2016

Channeled

From my Higher Self:

What is the purpose of this book?

Through this book, I am grateful to all of the energies, Elders, Spirit Guides, Archangels and Ascended Masters who, from above have guided my hand. Through this book healing occurs and anyone who reads it all, or even only parts, will in some way be healed. This simple book has been created as a tool for parents. It is to become part of the toolbox parents have to raise their children; may they be their own or someone else's they have accepted in their heart and life.

Channeled:

We have set to motion a series of shared wisdom, exercises and prayers to guide parents in this important role of raising their children. Parents and children have much to learn from one another as children are also teachers. Through this book, parents are given insight as how best to achieve this. Parenthood is not easy, as each parent and child bring with them their individual personalities and experiences. Through this book, parents will learn how best to heal their relationships, to learn and grow as equals, each on their respective path.

This channeled book is our gift to you as the moment has come for families to energetically connect as individuals to each other. We are all part of some kind of a family, the ones we are born into or the one forged out of necessity, as we seek for love in its purest form.

The world is ready for such a book, therefore we send it forth and ask you to trust in its wisdom as all parts of this book form a powerful tool for you to improve your family's lives. This is not necessarily a book to be read from front to back, but a book where you focus on an intention or an issue you are having, and open a page. You will always be drawn to a part of the book connected to you at the right time.

We ask that you place your trust in us, and that you choose to live your life connected to all energies which surround you. Mother Earth and Native Elders are forever present, and always eager to impart their blessings and sacred knowledge as you connect to them and to this beautiful Earth. Their energy signature is dense and watery, ebbing and flowing as tides do. Their communal heartbeat is strong, slow, and steady, allowing you to feel grounded and present right here, right now, on this beautiful Earth.

From Grandmother:

The colours, from which you seek healing energies, are the deep browns yellows, reds and greens. Focus my Child, as you feel yourself become one with the Earth Energies. Our energies will soothe you and rock you, as every fiber of your body gathers our strength and healing. Through your mind's eyes, see the web of veins and arteries in your body connect to the web, and with your feet firmly planted on the Earth, feel the energy flow, slowing down your breath as you connect to us, allowing the very deep energies of Mother Earth to channel through you, bringing you healing and peace, Dear Child.

From my Higher Self:

Breathe in and breathe out.
Allow
Breathe in and breathe out.
Allow

Continue to meditate on simply being in the moment and allow the healing to occur.

We are blessed as we consciously connect to Mother Earth.

April 15, 2017

Channeled

Life, as a warm summer breeze, brings promises of support and gentle guidance. We, who open our hearts can easily tap into this knowledge, center ourselves and learn to grow into stable, kind, and conscious beings. Beings who live in the moment, and who enjoy the beauty surrounding them. Accepting the daily challenges they get to live through as they mark us as individuals with specific DNA who, through nature, love, tears and laughter grow, grow and grow. By accepting the fact that we are energy beings, we can take the time to breathe and expand our energies, centering our thoughts on positive light and outcomes so we can live in a grounded way, every day. Nature surrounds us still, and is only as far away as the other side of the door or the window. It is always ready to embrace us, to nurture us and to support us if only we take the time to look up from our daily grind or the rut we feel trapped in. Regardless of the situation we face at the moment, albeit joyful or sad, we need to take the time to look up from the task or present moment and feel the Earth's motion and energies so we ground ourselves in the light of each passing moment. Today your task is to look up, to connect, to breathe fully and to smile at life.

Listen to Mother Earth and Spirit and be willing to try something new which is actually something very ancient which unites us all here on Earth and in the afterlife.

I breathe, therefore I am.
I feel, therefore I am.
I learn, therefore I am.
I am, therefore I am.

As channeled from my Higher Self

April 26, 2016

A personal comment about raising children: When children are young, it is crazy busy and, lack of sleep, keeps you in this go, go, go survival type mode. You worry if you are being a good parent, but your brain is so fogged up from being sleep deprived that your instincts usually simply take over. Then come the Elementary grades where your child is just like a sponge, soaking up learning at an amazing rate. The wonderful, funny, scary, crazy moments fill you with awe as your hope for your child is to develop qualities to become a caring adult. And then, the dreaded teenage years when one remains vigilant as well as caring but perhaps, at times, at a distance so your child can develop independence and confidence in their own individual skills.

The most important piece of advice given to me to navigate the teenage years came from an evening session called "How to talk to your teenagers", I took with Lori Wilson and one of her sons, Denver. He said, "Listen when your teenagers talk, whenever that may be". This was indeed the best advice ever as, with my own teenage daughters, many opportunities occurred when I least expected them or even wanted them, i.e. at my bedtime. These fleeting moments were doorways of communication which kept the lines open and allowed me, not only to set boundaries, but to learn about these great young individuals taking shape before my eyes.

Then, you have for me the toughest growth period, the transition into young adults where children are so busy studying, working, volunteering and seeing their friends. You feel, in a way, like an empty nester as no one has time to help out at home where you are left with all the responsibilities of cleaning, cooking, etc. Some of you will say that one only has to impose "the house rules" or ask children to pay rent as you are offering a service to keep them supported in room and board. Yes, I could have asked my daughters to help more but I could see how stressed they were at wanting to excel at it all. I could also see they had no real time and that they were stretched as thinly as they could be, without breaking. Therefore, I did not ask too much and was always pleased that, when they had time, they did offer to help. This made me aware that, indeed, they were trying their best under very difficult circumstances.

I know my daughters can clean, cook, sort, budget etc. but they also learned to manage their time, study, work to pay their studies as well as take the time to volunteer. This made me proud as, perhaps they could have done more day to day routine stuff, but what they were learning as young adults made them more complete individuals who have a kind heart. Not a bad lesson in itself. As I realized how much they actually accomplished and the real stress they were under, deciding to back off chores, allowed them to be more successful in the end. As for myself, I tried to do more but, at some point, I decided as well that I needed time for me to learn and grow so, perhaps the house was not in perfect order, but I can say my daughters are proud of their efforts and I of them.

Channeled

What is important in life you ask? It is the heart and how we show love and support to family, friends and others. How we allow ourselves to grow as we watch others grow. How beauty is in every simple step we take; every time we look up and notice beauty which surrounds us. A simple smile opens a wonder of opportunity, a chance to share, grow and learn just a little more each time. Love is a colour. Some say it is red and sparkly, but I would say it is the calm confidence of blues and greens of an ocean wave gently lifting us to new heights or forcibly propelling us to aim higher, getting a different perspective so we can set our sails in a new direction, following our heart's desires. Still the mind, open the heart and see what colour shapes your world, understanding that the colours change, ebb and web as the meanders of life propel us a little farther each day. Where will you go next? Does it matter? Your heart will take you and, if you surrender, your path will become clearly laid out in front of you. Navigate your heart's life to seek and find your true soul's purpose.

By my Higher Self

May 1, 2016

Note from my eldest daughter: mom this entry starts corny but gets better. –K

I remember my mom, my aunts, my beloved grandmother telling me to enjoy each day as, when we age, it seems that life goes by at an accelerated pace and that, with age, we realize all the wondrous things we are yet to see, enjoy, and live through. Indeed, we should always try to enjoy each moment as they are fleeting.

Note on today's task: I was feeling sore from preparing all the flower beds yesterday as I knew it would rain today and that, having removed all weeds, especially the forever creeping gout under my magnificent rose bush, plants would benefit from being healthy inside, as well as outside. However, among all of Sunday's business, I started to feel restless and unhappy yet again about what I had not achieved. So I decided to take a bath with Himalayan salt and lavender oil mix created by a friend of mine. My muscles were sore from the previous day and I thought a relaxing bath would help.

Before hopping in, I decided I needed a focus for my rest (talk about a type A personality!) so I pulled out three cards from Doreen Virtue's Life Purpose Oracle deck of cards. One card was the Speaker, who has much to share with others. The second card was Career Change and the third was Family. In the Family card description, it said to look at each family member and to forgive each one by holding the intention of forgiveness for them. So I did just that. It was interesting to me that, as I did this exercise, I felt myself relax and more at peace. I also decided to add myself in this forgiveness exercise and this allowed me to look at how much I had actually achieved over the weekend. The day spent in the gardens had really allowed me to live in the moment which is something I needed to be more aware of. We are all working so hard on a daily basis so today, try the above forgiveness exercise and give yourself a well-deserved pat on the back.

Channeled

I am the Earth deep beneath your feet.

I am the hot core of the Earth from which you ground yourself and from which you center yourself.

Feel its strength coming through your feet

Feel the tingles of your cells as they align themselves to the core of the Earth.

I am grounded and at peace.

The Divine Power of the Earth flows through me and, as I breathe, I shed.

I shed fear and doubt.

I shed feelings of inadequacy, anger and resentment at not having all of my needs met, at having to navigate through others' demands and requests for help.

I shed my feelings of feeling obliged to do certain things, to be a certain way. Instead, I ground myself through the core to the core of my own being.
I am now in the light of the sun as I energetically stretch to my full height, soaking in the belief that I am who I am supposed to be, who my soul recognizes as an old friend finally having come to stay.

I am, I am, I am.
I am at peace.
I am grounded.
I am a being of Light and Love.

Today, I simply am and I am grateful for this opportunity to connect to my soul and its purpose here, right now, at this moment, on this grounding Earth.

Have no fear of who you truly are as peace within is peace living.

From Rowan, a very old Spirit friend of mine

Draw a page of figure eights or Infinity signs to anchor the healing.

May 5, 2016

What wisdom will I channel today as I sit outside next to my majestic maple tree, looking over the new growth in my garden. I am home from school today as I have had very bad asthma all week and felt I needed to rest and let the medication work.

Dream state

There is change in the air. The Earth energies are strong as I write and a gentle breeze keeps me company. It is a day of rest as sometimes we need to sit still to recuperate but mostly to listen. New doors are gently opening, inexorably moving us forward. Standing at the doorway, we wait. We ask, "What do we wait for? The right time?" The right time is always when your heart says go, before the brain puts up all kinds of mostly unnecessary roadblocks, fears, doubts and questions, such as: What will others think? Am I really ready? A gentle bell chime tolls in my neighbour's yard and it is a lovely sound. It encourages me to still my mind and allow opportunities, thoughts, and desires to arise. I reflect on what I have achieved so far in my life, not only in a material way but spiritually as well.

Channeled

Sometimes, a quiet moment is needed to reflect on what was, what is, and what could be? What could be if I only opened the door a little further? Today is a day to rest, to stand still, to watch, hear and smell nature as it unfolds on this spring day. Regardless of the season, feel a large white cloud surrounding you, adding protective layers to moments you take for yourself today. In this grand white fluff of this energy cloud, feel the energies as they envelop and protect you, but also, as you feel the calm surround you, there is power afoot. Saturate your cells with these lighted energies. Feel the levels of each cell fill to its maximum, creating joy, understanding and peace within. Just still the mind as this process occurs, leaving you balanced, calmed and strangely energized for what lies ahead.

From my Higher Self

May 29, 2016

A few weeks have passed since I have had sufficient energy to channel in my journal. It has been busy as I try to sort out my life's wants and desires and continue to teach and do mundane but necessary house chores. However, on this beautiful Sunday morning, I woke up feeling such peace and calm that I feel the need, no actually the desire to write a few pages to see what my Guides have in store for me today. I am simply sitting on my patio, in awe of the beauty of my tall ferns in my garden. They are amazingly beautiful this spring. Their stalks are firmly planted, strong and sturdy. Their lovely triangular leaves sway gently in the breeze. It reminds me that I am grounded today and that I can allow the wind to guide me a little, pushing me gently toward new ventures and, especially to new people yet to fully enter my life. I feel at peace with what is to come, which is really out of character for me being a worrier and a planner. I will most certainly take the time to enjoy the moment as it is.

Both daughters are home now and my house is once again complete. My youngest was a supervisor for a high school trip out to a small Native community in British Columbia. As she was recounting her experience, I found myself in awe of her wisdom and clarity at such a young age. We are blessed to have each other in our lives and now I channel.

A channeled dialogue between my Higher Self and Grandmother

Oh blessed Mother, we give thanks.
You are old, but you are timeless.
You are serene yet in constant motion, gently cascading as waves to the shore.
You bring us ideas and grant us the knowledge to act upon them.
Trust that all is well is the key to change, the key to life's decisions, past and present.
The gentle breeze on our faces reminds us of who we were, who we are and of who we so longingly want to be again.
What is a life's purpose but to be?

To this, Grandmother responds:

Think on your life, but do not fail to notice the gentle breeze of the Spirits who continue to guide you, gently pushing you in a given direction which is your life's purpose.
If you stop and listen to the gentle breezes, there is no need for shattering moments where you find yourself at a huge crossroad.
It is true that when one stills the mind, the path shown or felt is the right one.

So, Dear Ones, let go of what you know and what you fear.
Trust the gentle breezes and follow what your heart shows you.
This is the path which will take you to your life's purpose.
Do not try to connect with your brain as this is not the way, but connect with your heart; stop and listen to the breeze.
Feel fully grounded through solid roots, but allow the rest of you to ebb and weave as the gentle winds speak to you.
Trust in the Blessed Mother as she will guide your steps, perhaps taking you in a new direction or perhaps one you already know and recognize.
Allowing yourself to turn and follow will feel so right in your whole body.
And, like a well-oiled machine, all will run smoothly.

Prayer to the choices I make

I still my mind

I am grounded on this Earth

I accept my path

I trust my Spirit Guides

I let go, follow the breezes and move forward

I know I am fully supported in my choices

My choices feel right to me at this moment in time

I take the time to stop and listen, to connect and simply be

My life is mine. I own my choices as they take me on the right path

I am at peace

I am at peace

I am blessed

From my Higher Self

May 30, 2016

Hope is a strange business! We hope for the present but mostly we hope for the future, for others, for humanity and again for those around us. Some people make their business out of the hope of others. Is this wrong? Is this right? Hope is an opportunity which each one of us tailors to our own realities. Having children, we live hope on a daily basis, trying our best to give our children what we did not have. Hoping they will be independent individuals, beautiful inside and out. Children hope so fervently and, as we age, we learn to hope with a certain dose of reality as some of our hopes have been crushed and others, which seemed reasonable and attainable at the time, now seem silly or simply out of reach. But still, we hope.

Hope is like having a sky full of shooting stars. Each wish unique and tailored to a need or a want. Hope is a necessary evil at times as we sometimes feel so down in the dumps that thinking of hope is difficult. Hope is, of course, not evil at all as it allows us to find positive outlook in our lives. It also allows for an openness of the heart as, if we dare to hope, things may yet change for the positive, for us all.

Prayer of hope

As you awake in the morning you take a new breath of a new day.

Take the time to breathe in and out a few more times, stilling your ever-eager brain to get on with your day.

Stop and notice:

How are you feeling this morning?

Look outside and notice nature.

Breathe some more and send up your hopes to the Universe.

Do this daily for a week and see if your life has shifted in any way. It may only shift a little but that is a step, a movement forward, taking you somewhere new, somewhere you may not have considered before.

A path opens. Do not be shy, take a step.

Who knows, you may find life eagerly awaiting you.

Channeled

Layers

I am Divine
I am Light
I am the colours of nature
Which one am I today?
No need to know why and analyze it all.
Just immerse yourself each day for a week into colours you see.
You may find that each day brings a totally different colour
Or that each day brings shades of the same colour.
No worry, all is well.
Find in nature a symbol which best represents this colour.
The symbol should not be difficult to think of or find.
Notice its outline, its feel, its depth, feel its layers.
Each of us has layers and, at different times in our lives, we require a few more layers as we feel a need to protect or cocoon ourselves.
When you are done noticing all of the beauty of your chosen colour, envelop yourself in it and feel cocooned for the day.
Enjoy this little exercise which is actually linked to hope.
As you release your day's colour at night, send it off into the sky as a shooting star, carrying your hopes for that day.

Light & Love, always

Disappointments.....

In life, we sometimes disappoint others through no fault of our own. My mom was visiting from Quebec City and, with my youngest daughter, we had planned to go to a beautiful beach two hours away. I had woken up feeling tired with an upset stomach but, instead of saying anything, I decided to push through and we left for the beach. Halfway there, after many stops, both daughter and mom said for us to turn back as obviously I was unwell and not up for a day at the beach. I felt deflated and upset that I had let them down, even though they were both supportive and kind about it all. I managed to get back home and sent them off to another water hole where they could enjoy nature and have fun together. I stayed home. I was glad to be home, but it took a while for me to feel really okay about the change of plans. Why is it that we often set such high expectations on a planned event when something simpler would have sufficed?

And to this, Grandmother says:

It is all right Child, do not fret. It is as it should be. The world does not stop turning or evolving because plans change. You needed to rest and that is well. The other people in your life on this day needed to re-connect in a way that you had no control over. Even though you tried very hard pushing through, in the end, it was not worth all of this effort on your part as life created a different opportunity for all; you to channel me and them to re-learn to be friends. Allowing a better understanding of how important they are to each other, the universe decided to remove you as an intermediary. Therefore, they could clearly communicate with each other, as their rhythms allowed. Communication occurs at its own time. Learning to be flexible and flowing with change is all part of life lessons here on Earth. There is always a purpose. That you see it, or even understand it, is not always necessary or even welcomed at times. Yes, life is mysterious to each and every one of us but, remember Child, that everything serves a purpose. You may not always understand it, but it is as it should be, so do not be upset by changes of plans, but embrace them as changes in life are always occurring as they should. So, Dear one, embrace life as it is, where plans change as, not following a predetermined path brings a rich outcome of discovery, about oneself and others, who accompany us on this particular day.

Be blessed and feel blessed on this special day.
Grandmother

July 21, 2016

I have finally committed to writing, finish writing and publishing this book. I had felt a little disconnected in the last few weeks having been on holidays, visiting family. It actually became very apparent this time around, that I hide behind a protective wall when I visit friends and family. I am not sure why I do this, and what is the purpose of it all as who benefits from me hiding who I am from anyone? I know I am a healer with skills to share. I know I can do so much more in terms of healing others than I currently do and, hiding, of course, stems from two possible thoughts: the fear of being judged and the fear of not being good enough.

I have really worked hard at not really caring about who judges me for who I am, but it seems to be harder with family who think they know us so well. It is also perhaps because they are our family that we feel they should always be the most understanding and encouraging towards who we truly are. But alas, often it is not that way, or more precisely, it is not the way our heart desires. Perhaps, it is in how clearly we express ourselves to them that makes the difference. Unconditional love and support are precious, rare, and often, as we get older, we notice that they do not necessarily come from our families, but from our friends and/or from others who are attuned to our frequencies. So, this brings me back to trusting my own healing abilities which, I have been told, are very much worthwhile, even important to this world, and that I should trust that I have great abilities to help others. In my deepest heart, I know this, but it has taken me years to open the door to being a healer, and subsequently, being who I truly am, so no wonder it takes some time for my family to get used to who I am now.

Being a teacher, I am a communicator, and I know I have the ability to express myself clearly for others to understand my message. Over the years, students have often said that, one of the things they appreciated about my teaching was the ability to explain a concept by breaking it down into parts or by explaining in many different ways. So when it comes to explaining who and what I do, why is it so difficult for me to achieve the same clarity? I think perhaps it is because it is me I am talking about, as my life and healing are not just curriculum concepts. I think in life, when we are faced with explaining ourselves to our loved ones, we need to order our thoughts as if we are teaching a skill such as tying one's shoes without using velcro. In refining who we are, by breaking down the parts, we can clarify who we are and what we truly want.

I know, when dealing with immediate family, we get into multiple layers of love, wants, guilt, hopes and fears all melted into one. No wonder we sometimes have a hard time sorting our thoughts and feelings to get to the naked truth of exactly what we want to say and how we want to say it in order that it is accepted or, at least, considered by other parties. I think if we took more time to break down our thoughts and sort through all emotions to only be left with the main ideas, the real essence of our message, we would be happier and, possibly, our messages would be better received. We often hear of family members talking about other family members having inadvertently hurt their feelings. We hear them say "I know they care but… I know they love me but…" We hurt our loved ones by how we sometimes express ourselves. Often, we do not mean to and, when told that we have deeply hurt someone's feelings, we regret our words and realize that, if we had segmented our thoughts and gotten to the core of our message, we would most probably have expressed ourselves in a less, hurtful manner. I will try to listen to my own advice. I realize it will not be easy as we are sometimes required to respond quickly to quell a situation we face, but perhaps, before we speak, and this, even in the heat of the moment, we can breathe deeply a few times. By doing this, we should communicate more effectively, but more importantly, we should communicate in a more caring manner. I think it would be worth trying. I am willing to give it a go. Are you?

Channeled

We love our children
We love them deeply and always try to be there for them even though, at times, imperfectly.

A family is a series of puzzle pieces which, periodically, really click perfectly together. At times though, a family's puzzle pieces don't truly fit as some corners have been overused, and some colours on some pieces have faded. But, those same pieces, once in a while, still fit rather well together, hence rekindling the joy of being together and understanding that each piece represents a different part of the full puzzle. Each piece having a role to play in order for the unit to be complete. Other family puzzles seem to have bits from different landscapes as the center pieces which, in turn, may try their hardest to steer all the pieces to fit as one master puzzle but, as they are ultimately from a different picture, they do not fit. The loose piece or pieces may feel like outcast or different, until life brings them to their own puzzle image from which they build, or to which other pieces join in.

A family will also have multiple pieces join and leave. They may have puzzle pictures, very similar in theme, growing side by side, and all is well this way. If you are born differently in a sea of similar pieces of one puzzle, don't worry as to the left, to the right, bottom or top, your belonging puzzle can be found. Venture a little if this is the case for you, and see if you can find your own puzzle image where you truly fit. We all belong somewhere and, when we are there, we know we fit perfectly, and the peace of mind that follows is magical and well worth the quest.

As a puzzle piece, it is important to identify your own shape, colours of your edges, and what you represent. This will allow you to quickly glance at other puzzles presented to you through the course of your life, to decide where you fit. We all fit somewhere safe where we are allowed to grow, learn and feel fully connected. Realize that there is no point in trying to fit into a puzzle that isn't yours, so stop wasting energies and feeling deflated, as if you look up, just over the horizon lays your shiny own puzzle with supportive pieces who welcome you as you fit oh so nicely with them.

From Archangel Uriel and Titus who lived in Roman times

Footnote: Oh wow! I am amazed and truly blessed to have channeled these two amazing Spirits. I am grateful to be learning so much!

July 22, 2016

Wisdom from our children

We have all heard the saying that our children teach us and usually, we get this. Then we forget and move on, but as I read my eldest daughter's advice she wrote on the last page of my journal (see below), I see that indeed, I need to reflect more on this true saying as we all possibly should.

Our children are younger than us in this lifetime, but I think and, perhaps it is often the case that, in Spirit lives, they are sometimes older and wiser than us. They are certainly here for us to help and teach them, raising them in the best way we know, but I think, if we are honest with each other, we see that we have so very much to learn from them as well. Our children or children of friends, colleagues etc. each bring an aspect of life we perhaps had never considered. As well, our children follow a different path than ours, therefore they show us life under a different light. But even more than that, they show us an array of new possibilities we might never have considered possible. I mean this in big, innovative ways by, not only changing the world for the better, but also, in all the little ways we can make our lives better.

We often hear when raising children the words "to keep it simple" for them to get it, but sometimes as adults we hear sayings such as "holding down the fort" or "drowning in responsibilities". This is especially true for single parents as we often find it difficult to simplify as we stress over too many scenarios of what could be, could happen and the "what ifs" of our lives, let alone to consider our basic needs of food, shelter and love. Children are happy playing with one toy at a time, thus showing us to focus on each task as if they were crucial to our lives and yes, this should, of course, include such mundane tasks as washing dishes.

I have often gotten a tarot card picturing women building a wall one brick at a time, focused on the task of building the said wall one step at a time. We all know that life as adults is far from simple, but if we tried to focus on one task, one smile, one lesson at a time, we would perhaps feel that indeed we are building something really worthwhile. Yes, this process will take time, but let us not be impatient and cross with our adult self for not being able to do it all at once. We should, as many wise beings tell us, live in the moment. Living fully in each moment, for you and me I am sure, is a task we need many reminders to achieve as, let's face it, change requires practice and awareness. So why not start today and really try to BE in the moment, one brick at a time, to really build something worthwhile and of which we can be proud of.

Wisdom from my eldest daughter as referred to at the beginning of this entry.....

Dear Mom,

Being angry at one another is a part of relationships. It does not mean that I love you any less and I know that it doesn't mean that your love has faded. It's okay to be frustrated with each other and I do think it's healthy to let the anger flow every once in a while. In addition, you cannot control everything that happens to my sister and I. There will be ups and downs but that is just the cycle of life for you cannot blame yourself when things go badly for us. We have our own lessons to learn, and these situations we face, do not reflect on you in any way. Do not blame yourself for all of it and do not feel pressure to fix all of it. Trust in us and in others, things will work out.

With love, Kimmaly

Channeled

I live, I love, I die
Where does the time go?
I live, I love, I die
What will I remember most?
Is it the pain?
Is it a smile?
Is it the colours of a garden in bloom?
I live, I love, I die

What layers will you place in between each main event of your life?
It is really up to you, what you choose to live and to learn.
I live, I love, I die

Decipher each verb repeated above and attach adjectives to them to truly
see how you want to live, to love, and to die.

Make a choice as it is all yours to choose
Set your feet firmly on the ground

Stand tall

Listen to your heart and choose.

Draw a page of figure eights or Infinity signs to anchor the healing.

From one of my many Spirit Guides, a very ancient and wise Native Elder gentleman named "Hoshowashee" of the Deer Clan

A Prayer for the little ones

May your life be blessed
May your hurts be few
May your failures teach you
May your happiness guide you
May your life be blessed
May you find kindness out of your struggles
May you find love in caring for others
May you find satisfaction in knowing you did your very best and listened to your heart
May you speak your truth from your heart, plainly and clearly, coming from a place of love and kindness
May you change the world for the better, little by little, action by action, gazing kindly at what surrounds you
May you learn from your Elders
May you learn from your peers
May you learn from your parents or from significant adults in your life
Listen, really listen to those who speak around you
Gather Knowledge and Wisdom from all you meet as each one has been purposefully put onto your path for you to learn who you are, what your heart holds true, leading you to your very own path in this lifetime
May your life be blessed
May your life be blessed
May your life be blessed from this moment on

One of my favourites.....

June 25, 2016

I am sitting down on my patio on this lovely evening as I listen to quite a few cardinals "chirping" away in the trees at the back of the yard. My daughters are at volleyball and I feel very peaceful as I write. I really do not yet know which of my Guides will show up today, but I am so very grateful to have been chosen at this point in my life to channel such extraordinary beings who impart their wisdom for all of us to read. Even though my Ego at times struggles with the concept of me actually writing a book, I have to sit back, relax, give thanks and accept what is coming through as important to this world, at this time. As a result, I am told by a Band of Elders to explain to you how I link myself to Guides/Angels or whoever decides to come forth on this day, to share their words with me.

As I write my little introduction on topics given to me, I feel connected to my Guides above my left shoulder so I know someone is there. I don't tend to see Spirit unless I have to, but I feel a warm and lighted presence. When this happens, I stop writing my part, sit back a little, close my eyes, open my left hand palm up to the Universe. I breathe deeply a few times, and then I tend to have to smile as I have entered "the zone". The zone is like a luminous cloud above my head or sometimes just behind my shoulders and head. Then, someone steps forth and I start channeling. Words come through very clearly to my left ear as I am right handed. I am kind of a bridge which is formed between the Spirit world and my journal. It is really cool to be witness to this as, even though I am actively hearing and writing, I, as Lynn, am still there in the neutral zone. I do not always know at first whom I am channeling.

For examples, some Guides such as Grandmother, have a very particular speaking style and a feel to their signature energy so she is easily recognizable. Other Native Elders seem to have similar intonation and speech patterns. Archangels and Angels seem to come through in a more formal pattern in the message they impart upon me. By formal pattern, I refer to the sentence structures and the tone of the language used as if, for example, I was writing a formal essay instead of a message to a friend. What I know is, as my eldest daughter Kimmaly said, what I, as Lynn, write is of a very different style than what I actually channel. She joked that I sound cheesy at times whereas the words channeled were so very well-written, seamlessly flowing that she knew with certainty that it wasn't her own mamma writing. I laughed so hard when she said that as I was happy to hear that there was an actual difference in style. This is important to me as I want others to notice the difference, as well as making them more able to be open to the channeled wisdom thus imparted. When done channeling an entry, I ask who the Guides were so I can write their names as authors. I thank them and I reconnect to my world in awe of what just happened through me. I don't usually read over what I have just written, except for the prayers which I love as they deeply touch me as I hope they touch you.

I have never really understood the fascination people have with Angels and, in recent years, they seem to have become very fashionable as decorations in houses as Buddha images seem to inhabit gardens as lawn ornaments. Being born and raised Roman Catholic and, even though, my beliefs are more linked now to the core teachings of all religions, I remember always being fascinated by images of Angels in churches. They were beautiful, sitting way up high in the clouds.

As life would have it, at the 2016 Hay House Summit, I "stumbled upon" Kyle Gray. As I was perusing the numerous speakers to choose from, I clicked the choice tab which stated: "Let the Universe decide" where it was luck of the draw who you ended up listening to. I found myself listening to Kyle as he spoke of Angels. It seemed to strangely resonate with me which was a surprise. At the end of the hour, he recited a "Thank You Angel Prayer" which I quickly wrote down. After the podcast, I thought I had nothing to lose, stood up, opened up my hands and started to recite the prayer. I had to stop in the middle of the prayer as I was crying. After a few tries, I was able to complete the prayer. I was thoroughly "downloaded" with more information for this book as I felt the incredible power of Angelic Love coming through me. I was feeling all the Angels around me as Kyle had spoken about and was truly in shock and in absolute awe. I have continued to say the prayer and thank the Angels often. My experience confirms that yes, Angels are truly around us, here to guide and help us at every step. Try it for yourself by asking assistance from the Angels. You have nothing to lose, but only support to be gained.

This new found Angelic connection made me realize that we have so many Guides and Spirits who have passed, as well as Angels who surround us every day, awaiting our awareness as we call upon them for help. I am a happy believer and my heart is at peace.

Channeled

And to this Angels say…

Of course, we are here.

We have always been here.

We help, we guide.

We put forth events for you to notice and be guided by, even though we know you may not always listen to us, we still remain there for all of you here on Earth.

We are old and so well depicted by the master painters of olde.

We are bound to Christ our Lord but, it is in his Divine Wisdom, we have learned if and when we exist on your plane.

It is that same wisdom and love we cherish you with when you decide to connect with us and to acknowledge our presence in your world.

We constantly seek ways to assist you in your sorrows and your sadness.

We wait for you to extend a hand toward us so we can fully help each and every one of you, regardless of current beliefs you may have.

We are old, older than the Earth itself and, sometimes our words of wisdom come to you in a cryptic way it seems, but if you stop and think upon the strong and deep feelings you have, breathe, open your mind and heart, this will make it easier for you to understand us, to understand our love and support for you at this very moment.

As you read these lines, stop, breathe, open your heart and mind to us.

We are there, always and forever, loving you, guiding and supporting you.

Call upon us by name if you wish and we will come.

Call upon us as a group and still, we will come.

We, Angels of Light and Love are always there for you.

Hear us, let us guide your steps towards your truest self.

We are here right now with you.

From a Band of Celestial Angels

Prayer: Calling Angel Support to Yourself

In every situation find beauty.

In beauty you will find us.

If, for example, you are in a difficult situation, concentrate on finding a beautiful object, flower, picture, whatever catches your eye.

As you recognize and acknowledge the beauty of the chosen object, call upon us and we will come protect you and/or send you words of wisdom through your mind.

Trust what you are hearing at that particular moment as it is us showing up with love and support for you.

Breathe and trust in our Love and protection and so it shall be.

Draw a page of figure eights or Infinity signs to anchor the healing.

PS: Before I channeled this entry, I was talking to my lovely grandmother who is quite religious in her beliefs but open as she does her "healing protocol" daily on her chakras allowing her to live and still be vibrant at 103 years old. At the time of this entry, we discussed the fact that she had never really believed when people talked how their Guardian Angels had stepped in to protect her friends from sickness, accidents, etc. Then, I channeled this entry and I had to laugh as I called her back to say that Guardian Angels, let alone a band of them, had come forth and, through me, were showing her that yes, they did exist and that they were here to guide, support and love us unconditionally.

And she laughed in actual delight and amazement....

July 26, 2016

I am sitting very comfortably at a picnic table on the beach at Long Point Provincial Park in Ontario, Canada. It is simply a most sublime day I am spending on the beach with my two lovely daughters who are, once again, frolicking in the water as they are truly born of the sea. The beach is not crowded today as it is mid-week. There is a strong east wind which creates beautiful constant waves which come crashing upon the shore. It is actually quite noisy but, strangely, I am at peace and simply happy to spend the day with my daughters. As I prepare to channel and open up my senses, I am simply met by this beautiful and very peaceful white light. I am asked to focus on the wind and the crashing of the waves. It is excited "Surfer Dude" who joyfully appears at my side. He is simply an ecstatic being I channel when I am helping someone who has suffered tremendously from trauma, child abuse or who is suffering from cancer or mental health issues.

Even though I call him Surfer Dude as he literally rides the waves of healing, I am not fooled as he is a tremendous healer. He is young, wears long Bermuda shorts and really looks like a typical surfer of the movies with long shaggy hair. He laughs a lot and his unbounded energy is very bouncy and alive. He always knows to come when I am in need of his healing powers, even often before I know a person I am treating is suffering or has suffered in their youth or adulthood. He directs my healing via wave sounds, hence why he is here today at the beach.

Some people need healing in the gentleness of small waves, removing hurt and sorrow, small pieces at a time. Other cases, much more severe, require the great crashing of enormous waves stripping crusted hurt from a person. He guides me through wave sounds I make with my breath. It feels quite ridiculous to me but I know how efficient it is as I have seen layers upon layers removed from a person's main shell, having eliminated through the process, sheets of black coloured layers. After a treatment with Surfer Dude, some people feel more empowered to face their realities and ancient fears which have ruled their lives for long periods of time. For others, it shakes them a little in opening their eyes, looking at their surroundings and seeing who they are, what they have and what they yearn to be.

Everyone who encounters Surfer Dude and is healed by him is changed and must make changes in their lives. It is not always easy, but he is amazing and truly a force of nature. Moreover, his laugh, when he comes in, prepares me for a difficult task ahead, but I know I must listen and complete the healing. Consequently, if you have such issues, go to the beach on a windy day or listen to a playlist on YouTube. Then set the wave sounds you want and imagine the layers peeling off you, one by one, or the cancer cells clearing away, one by one, and they will.

Surfer Dude originally hails from beaches in New Zealand and Hawaii. As the waves, his buoyant energies are endless, playful and their aim is always true.

Give it a try and heal yourself or heal others this way. He assures me he will come and help.

July 28, 2016

Recipe for positive vibe sending via distance healing

Often, when my daughters, friends or colleagues are struggling with an issue, have a big test or presentation, etc. I breathe in and out a few times, and focus my mind on the person I want to help. Then, I imagine the person surrounded by light and either focus my energies on the head or heart depending on the issue at hand, or a body part if it is being operated on, and I send light to the area. It doesn't take long and you can repeat the process as often as you feel the need. The trick is not to attach any fears and/or doubts on the vibes/waves you are sending. Remember, always center yourself first, through your breathing and mind focusing, and send away. I encourage you to try it if you have not already done so, as I guarantee it does work.

An example of this in my life, was when my eldest daughter was studying at Ottawa University in her first year. Periodically, I would send positive vibes to her and to her residence room. After a while, we became very much attuned to each other and I would help her calm herself before exams and presentations. After a few months of this, my daughter said that her friends loved coming to her room as they felt a sense of calm when visiting. Therefore I know this kind of energy transfer and mind focus do work very well. They are free and really help others. Don't forget to include your pets in this energy sharing as animals certainly feel it as well. But always remember to breathe through the focusing. Trust and let go.

Channeled

And they say....

Of course it works, and to start doing transfer of energy often. At first it may seem strange, but you'll get very proficient at it very quickly. Everyone can and should do this daily. It is like meditation, as it focuses your mind on the positive, so it is beneficial to others you wish to help, and to yourself as well. When you do this, you nurture yourself while healing others. You don't need someone's permission to do this for others as long as you send only positivity and love. By thinking of others, you allow your guides to support you, opening yourself to not only giving bubbles of love, light and protection, but you are also receiving the same.

So believe the experts, positive thinking for yourself and others does work.

Channeled afterthought:

(Yes, they have those as well it seems...)

We know this is not a new idea and most of you will have heard of it before, so explain to us why you are not actively doing this on a regular basis? It is simple enough for all of you to do, so please trust us when we say, it works.

This entry was channeled as "We": a collective of Spirits from the other side who, through Lynn here, ask you to commit to changing your lives one thought at a time or should we say, one very positively hopeful thought at a time.

Channeled (continued)

Many a life's moments are endearing and bring a splendid smile to our face. When you smile this way, capture the joy, the essence of life itself. When worried about a loved one or a friend, revisit that special life's moment, reliving it and feeling its joy. That my friend is exactly the essence, positive vibes you will be sending to help out your very cherished loved ones. Bask in the feeling, revel in its pure pleasure, smile away and send it on, daily. Do this many times a day and send on an array of beautifully created light. This amazingly strong beam of Love and Light will get to the destination you choose as you send it on. If no one you know is in need of such a light at the moment you send, just think of a name, known to you or not, and send your beam onto the energies. It will get to where it is meant to go. Perhaps you will hear of its impact and perhaps not, but know in your heart, that your good deed for the universe is done and, yes, smile, breathe and voilà! And bravo to you! You are a vessel of Love and Light and your source of Love and Light is infinite, so keep giving, keep sending. Keep living in Love and Light and you will feel/see the worries and burdens of your own life lift away, connecting you to your Higher Self and to the Common Conscience of all of us, Earth beings, Spirits, Angels and to the ultimate wisdom and grace we all possess and are meant to share daily with each other.

With love,

Alfonso Di Grazzi, an old Italian priest.

After thought and precision: "We" = actually one soul but two separate lifetimes. The priest Alphonso was also a Buddhist monk in another life and it is as both representations of this special soul's thoughts which came through me as two voices with one common perspective, regardless of each lives' specific faith.

July 31, 2016

As a parent, we know that the loss of a child is one of the most tragic and difficult deaths a parent can go through. There are many sayings such as "they were angels here on earth" "their lives, even though short-lived, had a great impact on all who knew them", or "it was their time". It must be so difficult to see your child suffer, repeatedly, as they battle rare diseases, cancer or those who accidently die or who are even murdered. These souls cross over very quickly as they had not left the thereafter so long ago. It is hard to rationalize such deaths, and even to continue to live after such a death.

Time, as for every death which impacts us, does help. But the death of a child takes a lifetime to heal, or perhaps, it never truly heals. I am lucky and thankful to have my two lovely daughters living with me. My cousin lost her son when he was twenty in a car accident. I went to the funeral in Quebec City as I felt a need to attend. At the funeral service, my family, who knew of my skills, asked if G was there. And I said no which I found strange, as in my experience, people who have passed away attend their own funerals. This made me wonder where he was. As my mother and I were driving home, I felt like he was stuck at the accident site which was in a village just outside Quebec City. So, my mom and I went there even though I did not know what I would find or see.

As we drove through the village I saw him. He was crumpled over the sidewalk where he had passed. I was told by Spirit to call my cousin, as her son wanted to talk to her, and ask for forgiveness as he had been partying and now found himself dead, deeply regretting this quick passing. And so, very, very reluctantly, I called my cousin. In one hand I held my phone and told my cousin I had her son's hand in my other hand and asked if she would allow me to channel him for her. Of course she said yes, and this was one of the most beautiful, albeit strangest moment of my life.

They both expressed forgiveness and love, made peace with each other, and what had happened to them. I was balling of course after I left them, as I knew he would then feel okay to cross over, which he did. I did not know I could do this, nor did I ever envision myself doing this either. So perhaps, if you are a grieving parent, find someone who, like me, can possibly connect you, as I know true mediums can.

It is peaceful to know that people who have crossed have achieved peace, even though they may have truly suffered during their short lives here on earth. The impact of their lives is what we need to cherish and remember, especially when, like today, an anniversary of a death comes to remind us, that we truly, deeply loved a human being, and that, regardless of how old they were, who they were, and how they died, they are now at peace on the other side, never very far away from us. Regardless of the circumstances of their passing, we are blessed to have known them as we cherish the memories we have of them. Yes, perhaps it was their time, but that never stops our love for them and their love for us.

Channeled

Oh Blessed Child,

You are here, even though you are physically not anymore.

Your memories, smiles and joy you brought to us, we will forever cherish in our hearts.

Even though you left earlier than we, as parents ever expected, we are thankful for your presence amongst us on this Earth.

We are grateful you chose us as your family as you knew we would be there to support and assist you as you needed it.

We are also blessed by your presence and thank you for your time spent with us.

From a collective of children on the other side

You are cherished
You are loved
Through memories we have of you
You remain with us always and forever
Now that we have crossed, we are the ones here with you, to support you, to live the rest of your life knowing that you did your best to help us, to guide us as we needed.
We know your love
We appreciate and recognize your immense and profound love for us.
We want you to live your life after our passing as, even though our time has ended, yours has not, and life is such a joyous affair.
Live life fully, live your life as though you live for yourself and for us.
We will rejoice as we watch you enjoy each and every moment in life, through pain and happiness as you are living.
We want to be witnesses to your life, fulfilled here on Earth, as we wait for you above, but also as we truly delight in all of your successes and fully lived moments here on Earth.
Know that we are with you still and always.
Be on the lookout for messages from us, as we are sending them to you as reminders of our bond.

We ARE blessed and so ARE you

Prayer for those who remain...

Know that I am well
Know that I know how much you loved me
How much you tried to show me your love
How much you tried to help me
How much you would have gladly switched places with me.

Know that I am well
Know that I know how much you loved me.
There is no need to forgive, as I am now Light and feel no pain or hurt.
There is no need to cry anymore, as I am whole and well
There is no need to hide and feel guilty when you continue to live your own life, as I am Love and Light.
My steps mirror your steps, and I even sometimes hold your hand, to encourage you to yet again, take another step.

Know that I am well
Know that I know how much you loved me.

I am well
I am Love
I am Light and whole

I thank you for your love, even though you may not have always known how to show it. I feel it now where I am and return it freely to you tenfold as you have the hardest path of both of us as you have stayed behind.
Rejoice and know that I am there with you
I see what makes you happy and smile
I am proud of your achievements as you would have been proud of mine
I know you know I am there with you with every step.
When you falter, it is now my turn to support you and my heart is singing with happiness when you accept my help.

Perhaps I was young when I passed, but know that, on the other side, I am strong and vibrant, and you can wholeheartedly rely on my strength, happiness and support for you here, now, and always.

I am blessed to have known you, but you as well, have been blessed to have been on my path.

We are energetically linked, so call upon me when you are in need for that is the role I have now taken.

Know in your heart of heart that I am well

Know in your heart of heart that I know how much you truly loved me

Know in your heart of heart that I truly love you.

Rest my dearest

Live my dearest

This is my wish and my hope

Love you always.

From Guillaume and his band of life loving Angels

August 1, 2016

Time flies! Already August and days are getting shorter. My phlox and white Veronicas are in bloom and I am starting to eat produce from my vegetable patch. A few years ago, I was given tools such as a circular saw and a jumping saw. I love tools, which I know seems strange, given the fact that otherwise, I consider myself a more conservative woman and mom as I love to cook and feel good/satisfied when a corner of my house is cleaned to my standards.

Two summers ago, I wanted to add a vegetable garden but did not want to spend too much money getting it done by someone else, so with my youngest daughter, we set out to measure and plan the area along the sunniest side of the fence in the backyard. Off to Home Depot we go, to buy long pieces of wood, unaware at that time that the people at Home Depot could have used their saw, at no cost to us, to cut our purchased wood…

Back home, I decided it was time to face my fears and use the saw. I put big boots on and I started the saw….. Oh my!! What noise and power it had! My first try, encouraged by my daughter whom I had asked to move well away, was quite shaky. I feared losing control of the silly thing and slicing away my foot, so I started cutting as fast as I could, at an almost unmanageable angle, to cut my first piece. I did not know the saw had a safety and that it would abruptly stop before the end of the cut I was making, so yes, I screamed and threw the stupid tool to the ground. After laughing and realizing that we were not hurt and that the first cut was actually pretty straight, we continued on, and after more careful measurements, we did manage to cut the wood as we wanted.

We mounted our pieces, and with our electrical screw driver, finished the garden frame. I can proudly say that, after ten years, my garden still holds and I am proud to eat the vegetable I grow. So what is the lesson here? Well, I think that regardless of what you try, it is important to see if you can face your fears. It is also the pride that one feels when something thought impossible, is actually achieved. Being a single mom, I could not ask my partner for help, and I did not really want to ask a neighbour or friend, who would have gladly come over and done it for me. I knew the garden project was actually something I really wanted and that I would need to put forth the effort at building it, as well as the effort at learning new skills, which I did!

Am I now the queen of the circular saw? Not at all, but I am a really good role model for my daughters, and that is very rewarding so I continue to challenge myself to teach my children, that even though life may throw many curved balls at us, we are able to face each challenge head on, and either succeed or fail. If we happen to fail, then we own up to it and ask our children for suggestions as how to fix the issue. As young or old, they do possess many creative ideas we may not have thought of. I am still proud of my garden and have gone ahead to learn how to fix and change a faucet, how to caulk windows, to change a bolt lock, etc. Through my years of being able to rely on myself, I have looked at each house problem I've had, and tried to fix it, with advice from friends, books and the internet "How To" section. Sometimes I failed of course, but mostly the job I did was not bad at all. There are no recipe books for raising children, so face each issue separately and notice what you are actually able to achieve. If that doesn't work, ask for an answer from your Guides and it will come. Of that, I am sure.

We all know that, it is from the challenges we face, that we grow into our true potential. If in all of our lives, we neither struggled nor feared, what would we learn? As many wise people have said, I too, am a strong believer that in this life, we are given the challenges we are able to face. This saying gave me the strength to deal with all that has come my way, and all that will come. I believe I am indeed that strong. Are you?

Channeled

Setting goals for yourself is very natural and a good way for you to focus on what you want to achieve in your life.

Life gives us small challenges to practise for the bigger ones we all live through regardless of circumstances and riches.

Although you may think the grass is greener elsewhere know that, although it may appear this way, it is usually not.

Even though the grand challenges in life can literally rip your heart, cause you stress and worry, know in your heart of heart that we surround you with love through these difficult times.

Know to look up and notice the rest of your surroundings and your life. All is never fully shattered as you remain alive and full of possibilities, hope being by your side.

Each one of you faces big moments in your lives. The purpose of these is to test your resolve to try again to improve and to change your outlook. The sooner you realize this, the sooner peace returns.

It will not be the same peace you perhaps had felt before, but it is a solid peace for where you are at that time.

Look up when feelings are hurt or when you feel like you are drowning. By simply looking up, you are telling the universe that you are ready for a change in your life, that you already see all the different possibilities which await you.

So please, there is no need to feel and be stuck; look up and you shall see what I see.

With so much love and trust in your abilities,

Archangel Julius, said the Brave

Channeled

Fear not, I am there.

Fear not, but instead look up and breathe deeply.

Feel the warmth and glow of your heart.

Perhaps it has dimmed in the slightest due to the many challenges you face but, by looking up, you have already begun to change your perspective, albeit a little.

That is great as this simple action enables me to surround you with great gentleness until you feel secure enough to move on.

I am very patient and will stay the course with you, enveloping you daily a little more at a time with such love and light.

Through my gentle hands and embrace, trust that I will guide you on the right path.

It may not be one you had considered for yourself, but trust me and let me guide you through this challenge so that together we look up and see what bright light awaits you.

But first, my dearest one, you need to take that very first step and be willing to look up.

I patiently await your readiness to take this step and, I realize how difficult this may seem to you, almost at times, to the point of being insurmountable.

But know that it is not really so difficult as once you have taken that first breath of change, you will find the right path.

Do not fear, God always rewards those who look upward from their current situations.

A clearer path awaits and I shall wait as long as it takes as, being from the other side, my sole purpose is to assist you in this transition.

I trust in you and the rightness you feel at your core as to which way your life will now head.

You are loved and supported as always.

Your Angel of Mercy,
Julius the Brave

PS: I feel so relaxed after having felt this amazingly gentle Spirit which came through for us all. The message came amidst layers and layers of love and calm. Thank you so much Julius the Brave for being with us today. I cherish this moment of moments and indeed, I am truly blessed to be such a channel of Light for all of us.

August 2, 2016

Channeled topic: Money

We all need it to live. Some have more, some have less, some have just the right amount to be happy. The difficulty lies in the understanding of what exactly is the right amount for each one of us. This amount may change as we go through the many stages of life, but it is our relationship to money that needs not change.

Green is a very vibrant colour, one that can be called upon to attract money. Simply stop a little, breathe and go within, finding the peaceful place inside yourself. The place where your mind stills and your heart is at peace. In this place, visualize all things green from moss to leaves of trees. Focus on the colour and see yourself surrounded by green. Do this exercise often, but remember not to attach any hopes and fears, wants and needs, to your vision, as this will alter the meditative benefits of such an awake dream. As you complete the exercise, continue to envision these soothing green energies and trust that what you need is already here, on this plane for you.

You may wish to find a green stone and put it in your pocket as you go through your day, reminding yourself of the beauty of green energies you have felt within your heart and soul. Trust in this exercise as it has already brought you wealth beyond compare. However, remember that the feel of time is different where I come from, so keep at it, and you will be pleasantly surprised at the results.

PS: This meditation is a transformative one, so allow sufficient time to really delve into the dream-like state it will create in you. Note that the green moss gathers at the Root Chakra

Channeled exercise to complete what has been outlined on the previous page:

Breathe and allow the energies to settle within you.
Breathe and allow.
Breathe and allow and, so it is.

Repeat as often as you feel you should

Please note that this entry is from a very very ancient energy who has no human form per se, but who cradles you as you call upon it.

He is named: Alarius Vittorio Victare
He hails from the energies of an olde Atlantis-like city seated deep within the Earth core, hence the Root Chakra connection.

Postcrypt from me:
I guess this message is for me as well, as I did wake up earlier today stressed out about money, and have been for the past week or so. I am spending more than normally these days, as I am instructed that it is time to invest in myself through this book which, I am told, will be very successful. So, let me find my moss green stone which I know I have somewhere and rest and relax, trusting that I too will be included in this bounty which has already arrived.

I do trust that all will work out for me, and for all of us in the end.

I am so very grateful

Being a single mom is sometimes really tough, even though I am very fortunate to have a great job I love, which helps me achieve my needs. My daughters and I are healthy and I know they will find their own path and be very successful in their careers as they already have an amazing work ethic, and a solid foundation, as they connect to their heart, mind and gut feelings when it comes to making decisions in their lives. I really thank the Universe, Grandmother, my Spirit Guides, Spirit Elders, Angels and Archangels who are guiding me through this process, and subsequently, through my life.

Merci! Je vous suis reconnaissante et me trouve choyée de votre bienveillance.

August 5, 2016

I have not written for a few days as life has taken hold of me, and daily chores and worries have needed my attention. But now, I feel a certain calm settle in and feel that it is time to sit, listen, and see who shows up to connect with all of us today.

A few weeks back, I was looking up Wayne Dyer on the internet and was scanning his tips and lessons. I came across one tip which stated that, when approaching a difficult situation or person, instead of worrying about the outcome and the actual meeting of a colleague or at a job interview, think upon the person you meet as though they are an old friend. This, he says, changes your outlook and your energy, making you more relaxed and positive. I thought this was such a great tip which I plan to use when faced with a difficult situation or person.

The more I thought about it, the more I wondered if this principle could actually be applied to family. I was so curious that I tried it out. All I can say is that the discussion I needed to have, went much better than anticipated. Moreover, I would say that the biggest change was how I felt before, during, and after the exchange. I was confident about the positive outcome as I was much more relaxed, which probably really helped the situation resolve itself. Transitioning with our children from stage to stage, child to tween and tween to teen and, the biggest for me, from teen to young adult is never easy as, not only do they themselves change and adapt, but so must we as well, change and adapt. We have to adapt as otherwise, relationships break and fall apart. So, when you have to discuss important issues with your children, siblings, parents and friends, think of them as really good friends and then, enter the arena. You will find perhaps, as I have just found out myself, that yes, things can go well and issues you worried about, can more easily settle themselves

Give it a go and see for yourself.

Channeled

When faced with a problem or an issue to be resolved, think first about the big picture and where the issue sits amongst the full lifetime of the person this issue impacts. How important is the issue in the scheme of one's life? Will it have a lasting impact? Who is it important to? If it is yourself, then you need to ask yourself if this issue really belongs to you or to someone else in your life. If it is someone else's, then release it to the Light. Be there to support the person if they are dear to you, but know that you can detach yourself from the final outcome and from the decision made by the other person.

If, however, the issue is yours, then you need to do a little thinking, but what is most important, is that you look at it through your heart's eyes. So breathe, focus and let your heart lead the way to solving this issue for you. Your heart knows the importance this issue has and/or should have in your life. Your heart knows the place, large or small, it should take in your life. Trust your heart and then, let go. When your mind wants to rekindle the interest you used to have for this issue, notice and acknowledge what you are doing, breathe and then let go.

This process will not be an easy one at first but, as you practise with the big and small issues of your life, you will find yourself more easily able to let go, release and refocus on the amazing aspect of your life. This will allow you to lead your life with much more positivity and isn't that, what we all yearn for?

DC

Channeled (continued)

A moment in time is only that: "a moment in time". Some feel like lifetime, and others are too quickly over. We attach life lessons, stresses and deep emotions to these moments, but truly, they are only and simply the moments which link together, create a full life. So, what kind of moments are you creating today in the links of your life? What will you be remembered for? What will you remember most at the time of your passing?

As you face each issue which arises in your life, reflect upon this. Is this truly an important link you want to attach to the others, or is it simply a passing difficulty which truly does not need to exist in the linked master blueprint of your life. Choose wisely, but remember to always breathe, still your mind, look inside your heart, and let the genuine thought come to the surface. By repeating this exercise, you will become much better equipped at choosing the real moments by which, at the end of your life, you will recall with fondness and peace.

Namaste
DC

August 6, 2016

Compassion and Support

If we have children, we love them. Sometimes, we demonstrate our love for them well and, at times, we find it difficult to express our love in a way that is understood, and even sometimes, acceptable to the person we love. As parents, we do our best and we make mistakes which we should own up to. Sometimes, we even need to apologize as, perhaps, we were clumsy in how we demonstrated our caring. The important notion is that we learn and grow as our own children learn and grow. It seems that for some people in our lives, it is easy to show compassion and caring. For others, it doesn't seem to be as seamless. I wonder why that is? It is not that we love them less but it is perhaps, that we love them differently, as we are simply showing our support and love in various ways. I think it all goes back to the original intention you have in the first place. This is difficult, at times, for siblings who are always so keenly aware of how their parents love them. As each child is an individual, each parcel of love and support given, is tailored to that person, hence different.

Uniqueness is a gift

You may find it easier to converse with one child as you share common interests and activities. But, for another child who is different from you, there is still a great need to show love and support. Therefore, you should not raise your children the same way as they are different individuals with specific needs. One child, for whatever reason, may need you more consistently than another. When this happens, you need to make a point of spending quality time with the other child, even if it is a five-minute conversation. This will have a positive impact, and rebalance the perception this child has of your love.

When raising my girls, who are very unique individuals in many ways, I have strived to show my support toward them, equally, always trying my best to tailor my guidance to each, individual personality. It is not an easy task, but as I watch my daughters, now, young adults, I know they have felt my love for them. I know this in how they treat others, and themselves. My girls and I are still learning and bridging the road of communication, and respect of our own individuality. A road which has taken us from their late teens to young adulthood where again, we continue to maneuver on a path which is not always clear to us.

It is really well worth the time and effort, to find ways to show your love and guidance, as now they can return the favour and be there to support and love you, when you're in doubt. They can even be there, when you have to make an important decision in your life. The growth transitions from being a child to adult are really never easy, and do require awareness, keeping your own desires for their future in check, so they can themselves find their own path. They will fail as we do. They will face heart-wrenching decisions as we do, but they will also love and learn. They will feel what it is to become an adult, as by going through the main stages of life, they are selecting their own path.

It is a joy and a wonder to watch our children grow. As parents, it is so thoroughly crushing to see our children suffer and learn hard lessons. But, we will get through this, as the love we share adapts and renews itself, as we grow older.

August 7, 2016

Channeled

Compassion is the world's best, and most effective currency.

Love is a grand emotion, a grand feeling of absolute proportion. In the Spirit world, love is all-encompassing and pure. It is the vehicle which allows all things to be created and shared. It is life itself and should be revered as such. Human beings sometimes use love as a bargaining tool which is not the purpose of love. When you have children, love should remain at its purest form, thus creating joy around you. When you try to box-in love or make it fit in a certain way, it fails as it should, as love cannot be boxed-in or tailored to a person's needs. Love is simply that what it is: love, the grandest flow of energy anyone will ever encounter.

Love is not to be used or even measured. It is meant to be shared and felt. Through love, all problems will be resolved, all differences will be put aside, all humans will grow into peaceful beings, radiating this pure energy. Feel its strength. Feel its serenity and calmness. Allow this serenity to ignite all fibers of your being, ensuring that all you subsequently touch, will be impacted by the love which surrounds you, and which surrounds all human beings.

Do not doubt this beautiful energy that is love as it is there for you to harness on a daily basis regardless of its form; may it be parental love, sibling love, partner love as any kind of pure love is truth. You should rejoice much more often in the energy of truth, which is pure love.

When you are loved, your being at its core is transformed, and peace within, is felt in its absolute glory. Human beings need to stop and connect back to the source of love more often, as it is from this source that all issues fall apart. From this source, that the difficulties you feel you need to face, leave your Spirit as no longer needed, or seen as truth. Love is the most powerful energy, so do not feel alarmed when it overtakes you, but trust in its purity, and know that it will guide your every step.

Archangel Michael

Heart choices versus the comfort of status quo

As I watch my small dog, Sydney, settle into a nice new plush blanket, I smile as who can truly resist a soft landing in comfort. Having been a single mom forever, people sometimes ask me why I never really dated and why I never put myself first, from time to time. I am not sure, as due to the circumstances of my divorce, I was the sole custodian of my daughters' lives. Perchance also, because of my personality, where I like to do things really well, one at a time, or perhaps, it is a combination of my personality and my job as a teacher, where one is always trying to help others. I think it was more simply a choice I made, from some guilt of having moved my daughters from one continent to another, at a very young age, and also, because I did struggle when I came back to Canada to settle myself and my daughters, into a set routine, that I did not want nor dare rock the boat again.

Whatever the reason, people sometimes remark that I should have missed having a partner, and, of course, a male figure for my girls. Maybe I missed out and did not notice the opportunities, as I was so focused on doing a great job at everything already on my plate, or at least, tried to anyhow. Did I miss out on physical touch or companionship? I would say yes and no. I was not living alone and received and gave many hugs and kisses in my lifetime. My girls and I shared many snuggles which seem to have sustained me for many years. Or, let's face it, my lack of a companion might simply be that I am too independent or afraid, but in all honesty, I don't feel as though I have missed much as it was ultimately an actual choice I made.

Now that my girls are twenty and twenty-two and have their own boyfriends, they wish for me to relearn the joys of companionship, and I must say, they are not incorrect in feeling that a door for me is slowly being reopened. Maybe you are like me, and have made the choice to remain on your own for a while, or perhaps you are one of whom they say always needs someone in their life. Whichever you are, look beyond the reasons of your logic. Look to your heart and face the hurt you have lived through, to be in balance, as everyone needs some form of companionship. I think this process has taken a long time for me to sort and heal. I made choices as we all do, but now, it is perhaps a good time for me to step into a different path. What about you?

August 7, 2016

Channeled

From love comes compassion and support, which are love's most trusted allies as they assist us in navigating the meanders of our own life. As we express compassion, we feel a renewed sense of purpose, and thus, our life is exponentially enriched. As human beings, it is in our truest nature to support and show compassion, for all who live here on Earth. Without it, our planet would have already crumbled to its core. But love is a survivor as, even though a person's life may have been filled with the most excruciating pain and loss, individuals are still able to show love; may it be towards animals, plants or other fellow humans. That is why we must live on hope, as hope creates passion and love.

When we feel loved, we feel much more solid regardless of the difficulties we encounter in our daily lives. We want more, and loving oneself starts a chain reaction around us, which enables those close to us, to feel its power and solidity. Don't be afraid to start this very positive chain reaction, as you will be amazed as to where it will take you, and how it will change and help those you surround, feeling supported in such a way to bring more joy in each and everyone's lives.

Chain reaction are two words often used to describe a negative, but here and now, start your very own positive chain reaction by surrendering to the energy of love we all have inside. Make decisions, or do not make decisions, is not as important as allowing life to unfold. Life will always unfold in the way it is supposed to, creating opportunities of growth and learning. When worried about a child, remember to always allow life to unfold as it should be, regardless of your own logic.

When your children are younger, they need you to be present in their day-to-day life, providing food, shelter, and some activities for growth. When your children are teenagers or young adults, your influence comes in spirits of teaching moments, so be aware of these and allow

How to Raise Your Children with Wisdom and Awareness

your child to make his or her opinions heard. Being heard is the first step to developing a more adult relationship with your children. And, yes, at times, you must be the adult making the final decision for the good of the child and family, but always allow your children to express themselves. By doing this, you are creating a solid partnership on which to build a more harmonious link for your shared future. So now, it is your turn to see how you can take this knowledge imparted here, and start applying it, regardless of the difficulties you sometimes have to communicate as a family, as the end result, will be a much, more balanced life for all.

Sainte Celeste

71

Draw a page of figure eights or Infinity signs to anchor the healing.

Evening of August 7, 2016

Archangel Gabriel is here to impart knowledge, but I am too tired to channel, and my eldest daughter needed to toss some ideas around, so I spent some time with her instead. I am sure Archangel Gabriel will catch me later and I thank him for his understanding.

The next morning, I try again:

Life of a parent

As stated in one of the entries at the beginning of this book, the best advice I had received to navigate the teenage years was that it didn't matter the time of day, but when your teenager opened up, it was crucial for you to simply drop everything to sit and listen as this was a golden opportunity not to be missed.

Many a time when my daughters wanted to talk, it was not convenient for me as it was often when I was just about to shut my light to go to sleep. However, I must say that Lori's son was so very right in his advice. I thank him as his suggestion permitted me to really keep the conversation open at a time when teens are learning who they truly are, who their friends are, and what they may possibly like to do when older. These are formative years and remember to take the opportunity of any window of communication which opens up to you. Drop everything and listen. You will be amazed at what actually comes out of these conversations, and the insights you gain from your teen on his or her life. These snippets of conversation will keep the communication thread flowing. They will also reassure your teen that, indeed, you are there for them which is so important in this daily life as today's teens' lives are bombarded by much more than we ever had to deal with at their age.

Channeled

Even though most people think children are simple beings, where adults are able to mold them by developing routines, activities, challenges for them to grow, note that they are complex beings who require a gentle touch. They may challenge us, become demanding, but that is only because they are trying to learn as quickly as they can. As parents, your role is to slow the learning process down and allow growth from within, through a multitude of experiences, joy and sadness. These are as important to your child's development as learning to read and write.

A well-balanced child is one who has a parent or friend who is a constant guidance in their life. A child needs that one, special person who will wholeheartedly listen to them, accepting their ideas and feelings, validating them, even though the child may need to be guided in a different avenue in the end. By listening, you are teaching the child that their voice is worth listening to, that they matter which, in the end, is what we all want in this lifetime. So get ready to create these opportunities to talk to your child.

Technologies must be put aside on a regular basis as the adult human is still the key to communication. If you have been in the habit of giving your child an iPad, computer, or phone on which to play, do not be fooled by the enjoyment they receive from these technologies, but take back the lead and remove the devices on a regular basis to create moments where actual, real communication may occur. This, in a world where technologies are so prevalent, may be difficult at first, and tears may be shed or tempers may flare, but persevere as it is crucial to your future relationship with your child to create these very precious moments.

If you are not as fortunate to have all these technologies around you, but are a parent who needs to work two or even three jobs to make ends meet, it is still up to you to create these moments to simply be and allow in your child's life. You do not need to spend enormous amount of time, but your efforts need to be consistent. Be there. Really there and you will be amazed at what you both learn.

From a Female Spirit with very bright green energy.

August 9, 2016

A day at the beach

I am again so privileged to be able to go to the beach with my daughters on this beautiful, sunny day spent on Lake Erie's shores. The sun is shining. The waves are just the perfect height to float on, and the water is warm and refreshing on such a hot, summer day. Children are playing in the sand and couples are walking by. Being at the beach is a privilege and it makes magical memories of time shared together, in a natural environment. I am so very grateful for this beautiful moment and I am fully savouring each breath of fresh air, all senses open, extended and extending.

Of course, Surfer Dude has joined us again as he is the king of the waves whether big or small, but Mother Earth also extends her warm welcome as she cradled us in her embrace. Water, in any form, is healing, but the most effective healing occurs in and around moving bodies of water. As we let water envelop us, we can shed our fears, doubts and worries replacing them with love and hope.

Channeled Exercise

Let your body sink into the sand on Earth, allowing yourself to settle into Earth's energies, adapting to its slower beat. Slow and steady as the beating of a lone drum. Feel the Earth beneath your body. Bask in the deep abyss which is slowly being created around you. This abyss is huge energy-wise as it cradles you deeply, on and around you.

As you sink deeper and deeper in Mother Earth, feel your heart and mind become one with the core energy gathered inside Mother Earth. Breathe in and out slowly, multiple times until you feel you have achieved the dream-state which stills your mind and which allows your body to recharge and rejuvenate at, and from this Divine Source. Remain this way until you have gained an innate amount of energy which will carry you through until the next time you allow yourself to be present near a flowing body of water.

Now say this:

I am at peace
I am now one with Mother Earth
I feel the Earth's browns, greens, yellows and reds remove all negative energies from me as I allow my breath to sigh deeply into Mother Earth. I am now fully immersed in this vast, soothing pool of energies, shedding old skin such as all of my doubts, worries and fears for myself and others I love and care about.

And they continue on:

As you shed, feel your nakedness and become eager to take on new clothes, ideas, ultimately a new skin, cleaned of all fears, doubts and worries. This new skin allows you to re-emerge anew, ready to once again take a few more steps into your own unique path. The one which you clearly see now as your own.

Your way is alight again and Mother Earth encourages you to proceed with your head held high, full of new found wisdom and passion for your own life, as it unfolds in front of you.

Go forth. Go now.
Feel whole and free.
You are renewed and rejuvenated once again.
Go forth. Go true.
Be blessed on your unique journey.
Mother Earth will remain, making her endless energies available to you as you need, Dearest One.
Always return when you feel you need to unburden yourself.

The Earth energies are endless, therefore you are always a welcome sight as you sink over and over again, deep into the browns, greens, yellows and reds of Mother Earth. She is your constant Source, so return as often as needed as your path is an important one, and we are always there to support you in the challenges you face.

Be blessed, Dear Child

From a band of roaming Elders who share the truth, the simple truth behind all of Nature's blessed energies.

August 10, 2016

When I started writing this book, I did so because I finally trusted Grandmother's advice to write, and because I had done a lot of work on accepting myself for who I am. I had gained greater confidence, and was starting to accept what my specific abilities were. I diligently wrote and channeled as I could. Now that I have made headways in this book, I find that I am starting to doubt myself again. I reread my last entry written at the beach, and feel that my writing of the channeled wisdom needed much editing in terms of grammar, sentence structures but, obviously, not the content.

This is disappointing to me and, perhaps I am quite tired tonight and should sleep on it. However, I really wonder why I still doubt, even though I was told to write this book, was given the main topics, themes, and reassured that it would be successful. I am very aware of how truly lucky I am to, not only get encouragements from family and friends, but that I am receiving so much support from all Spirits and Guides I have channeled so far. Even with all of that incredible and consistent assistance, I still find myself doubting that, in a few minutes or tomorrow morning, a wise Spirit will be able to find me again and continue to convey more words of wisdom for all of us.

I really wonder why I or anyone doubts so relentlessly. It is not that I had such a different childhood than many my age. It is not that I was unable to surmount challenges life threw at me so, why then, do I continue to doubt? Perhaps because I have embarked on a task which is so out of the ordinary for me.

Perhaps also, it is because that by writing this book and committing to actually publishing it, I am putting myself out there for all to see who I truly am. I know in my heart of hearts that I am done with concealing the real me which I have been hiding for most of my life. I know I have hidden my skills partially by choice because I am a single mom who needs a good job (which I still deeply love) for obvious financial security.

I think, perhaps, it was somewhat easier to present a one-sided persona to most people I interacted with on a daily basis. I also think I was giving my daughters the chance to adapt to the fact that their mother was a little more different than they had originally thought. I am not sure which is the real reason or if it is not simply a good combination of all of the above.

I think children need to know that, even though their parents are older, have more life lived behind them, they still struggle at times with, not only discovering their true path, but in finding what the best expression of this said path is. We all know no one is perfect. Children are changing beings who, not only have the hard task of learning who they are, their wants, likes and dislikes until they acknowledge their true nature and their most profound desires to ultimately lead their lives as adults. Perhaps when we doubt and reassess ourselves, we are simply taking a hiatus before we move on with our lives. Hopefully, after the pause, we are able to trust our hearts as we have allowed uncertainty to open doors instead of fearing and shutting down all avenues.

As parents, we must continue to strive to better ourselves to become great leaders and role models for our children. Maybe that is why we immerse ourselves in doubt. So we can stop, take stock of what we have already achieved so far, look at all the mistakes we have made as well as the wonderful things we have done, and find in them the courage and the force to continue on our path. I encourage you to share your doubts with your children as it is important to show that we are all searching for answers, regardless of our age, and life experiences comprised in our journey.

Therefore, tomorrow, and all other days until done, I trust that more great wisdom will be channeled through me until completion of this book. I continue to gain confidence that I am a worthy vessel for such a task. I also firmly believe that there is a greater purpose for this channeled wisdom than simply enlightening myself, my immediate family and friends. I trust Grandmother's clear knowing of where my path lies. I trust that I will be shown and guided what else is needed at this time in the world to impart even more wisdom from above to finish my book. I trust in the almighty wisdom of the many Spirit Guides to whom we are so grateful, and of which, we are in awe of what they have deemed important to share with us in this lifetime. I consciously remove all barriers of my mind and I find joy in trusting the powers-that-be.

August 11, 2016

Our youth molds us but it is in adulthood where we find our greatest challenges and where we have a choice of growing into caring individuals. There are many wise choices in this world now as we become more conscious of the healing energies that surround us. Healing for us all is not currently such a difficult journey as we may perceive or feel like it is out of reach for most of us. When we connect to the heart, to the Source, we are reminded that the choice is ours to connect on a daily basis and find peace within. So why not choose this?

Channeled

Doubt is a double sided coin, a positive and a negative

Positively, doubt is what keeps us safe as it allows us to be mindful of situations where we could be in trouble. But the negative aspect of that keeps us stagnant in our lives as it paralyzes our will to move forward or to look clearly at a situation from the perspective of the heart within. When doubt starts to cloud your heart, simply stop, acknowledge the feelings of doubt you have at that moment, and then set them high into the Light. Do this consciously and with purpose.

After you have done this, take as many deep breaths as you need and look inside again. Truly and without any other emotions attached, look deeply inside yourself. There you will find the strength you were perhaps aware you had, or this will be a new discovery of your own strength for you. Regardless of new or old healing, this very powerful strength of your core liberates you, strengthens you into being who you truly are.

Mind the outward distractions, keeping them at bay for now as you breathe in and out. In and out, noticing how the Inner Strength move from a central point inside your body to a glow encompassing your whole body. Breathe in and out a few more times. Each time relaxing out of your body the tension you feel and hold in your body on a day-to-day basis.

Breathe and release.
Breathe and release.
Exhale deeply and let go.
Again, breathe in.
Exhale deeply and let go.
Repeat as dictated by your intuition.

Channeled (continued)

By repeating this exercise, you will start feeling lighter, happier as your inner peace transcends from within to the outward consciousness of your whole being. By repeating this exercise daily or even multiple times a day, you will become aware of a great change in you, where doubt is finally at bay and where, within yourself you will find your strength, seeing the deep connection you have to your soul and to your Inner Wisdom.

So why choose anything else as, all you need to be, to truly be you in life, you already possess so connect, connect and reconnect by connecting to your true self which will make all exterior decisions easier to take and where you will have the detachment necessary to continue on your individual path, knowing that those around you will, in time, notice the changes in you. You will feel happier and more at peace. So now, when in doubt, know that you have the key to connect to your true Heart of Heart.

Namaste DC

Draw a few rows of figure eights or Infinity signs here to anchor the healing.

Channeled dialogue on doubt with Grandmother and my Higher Self

Never doubt, Dear Child, as when you doubt, you think you are alone.
Never doubt, My Child, as you are never alone.
We, the Ancient Ones, are always within reach. Always eager to support you and always eager to be called upon to support you.
Quiet your mind and you will feel us there through nature, even within big cities by looking, truly looking at nature for soothing energies and wisdom.
Doubt no more, my Child
We are here.
We are always here.
We surround you with the energies of Truth.
You are only to seek us to find us.
We abound and travel great distances when you call upon our wisdom.
Find a piece of green grass on which to firmly plant your feet.
Listen to the calls of the birds.
Listen to the wind in the trees.
We abound and travel great distances when you call upon our wisdom.
Close your eyes and stand still.
Feel the silence envelop you as it sets a veil of peacefulness within.
Do not doubt yourself and do not doubt us, Child.
We are where we have always been: close to your heart, offering wisdom and serenity at each and every breath you take.
You only need to call upon us and be present with us, through your deep breath and connection to nature.

Doubt is an emotion of your kind.
Yes, indeed, sometimes it is useful as it keeps you safe, but mainly, it is an emotion you should simply set aside as it does not serve your deep purpose on this Earth.
As parents, you doubt and create doubt in your children.
Doubt is not the same as profound conversations and discussions which are necessary as a means of communication of a family.

Doubt creates fear which supports no one. Cast it aside as it no longer serves you or those around you.

By trusting your heart, you will not feel the need to doubt as you will simply be.

Says Grandmother

By being in touch with your core, regardless of your age, child or grown, you will live your truth as your truth will become your own beacon of Light which you will clearly follow and be able to follow as your path is now your truth.

Let us all find the Light and feel the great support available to us and walk on.

Light of Light
We are one
We are all beacons of Light.
We walk our paths, side-by-side, knowing that if we need support, we are there for each other.
Our paths in life are interconnected, may they be far or close by.
If we truly walk our path, we see clearly what is, what was, and what lies ahead for us.

As parents, we are privileged to walk closely to the path of our chosen family members. If, in Light and walking our true path, we can offer support as needed but we should remember that each individual walks his or her own path, and it is not our role to take over another's path.

So be true and walk your own path regardless of the desire you have to control another's path. Attempting this never works and creates non-clarity as paths become needlessly intertwined. It is hard enough to steer your own path without taking on another. Support your loved ones, but also support your own truth and path. Yes, we walk alone on our path but we are never far from others who can, in turn, support us or be supported by us.

From my Higher Self

August 13, 2016

When a child is ill, lay your hand to heal.

We are often at a loss when our children are ill. Most of us have learned through trial and error what works best for each of our children, as not all medicine is created equally for the specific needs of each individual child. For instance, the only way to tell if my daughters had fevers when they were little was not always in their behaviour, but it was how glossed over their eyes were. So each child has his or her own telltale signs of illnesses. Mostly though, we are always thankful that most illnesses are short-lived.

As a child is sick, the mere presence of a parent is often the most comforting, and it is true that it is in the small gestures, such as making sure there is enough chicken noodle soup or that medicine is taken as prescribed, that a loved one is usually soothed. But, energetically speaking, one of the ways to wait out an illness can be to use the healing energies our hands possess. You do not have to be a full time healer to heal. Your love is healing and the energy flows through your hands to help relieve pain in a sick child. The trick is to have pure intentions at the heart and before you use your healing hands, connect to the healing energies of whoever from above happens to be there to help. Yes, believe me, someone is always present to help us.

Focus on pure healing which is simply to make your child feel better as you gently lay your hands to heal. You may touch your child or simply place your hands just about one inch above whichever area you feel needs healing. Breathe in and out, becoming the vessel from which healing energies from above transfer to your sick child. Do this for a few minutes and rest. Repeat when you feel the need to. This will work wonders and, remember not to attach any thoughts or fears to your healing. Simply still your mind, become the vessel and allow the energies to flow freely through you, and sure enough, they will.

Channeled prayer to set the tone for being a healing vessel

I ask that through me, the healing energies from above transfer to my child.

I ask this from a pure heart.

I trust that all that transcends is pure and loving.

I am one with the energies.

I accept that, without a doubt, they flow through me to quickly heal what ails my child at this particular moment.

I trust in Love above.

I am grateful to become the vessel through which all necessary healing will occur at this very moment.

As I link the energies from above to my child, I step back from worries and allow.

As I allow the healing energies to flow through, I as well feel uplifted and give my worries and doubts away, feeling refreshed and renewed as I continue to take care of my child.

As a result of this gentle and peaceful exercise, my child's health improves.

I trust myself enough to give the healing commands over to the ever healing and powerful energies of the most benevolent healers from above.

I trust
I allow
And so it is.

Draw a page of figure eights or Infinity signs to anchor the healing.

August 14, 2016

I have been asked today to write about and/or channel a description of the feel of Heaven's energies in comparison to Earth's energies. Earth energies are an integral part of this book and are represented through Grandmother, respected Elders and Mother Earth herself so please refer to those entries for the feel of earthly energies. I would also like to point out that one is not better than the other as both are amazingly healing and serve a great purpose in supporting us. Link to whichever group of energy you feel you need at the moment, and trust it will be the right one.

Healing from above for me is more in my head space as it feels like bright clouds on a sunny day.

Channeled:

It is like cotton balls and lightly comes to envelop you, gently cocooning you in soft light which, at times shines, also very brightly above your head. As the light and energies envelop you, feel its inner calm settle on your soul. Feel its healing take over your head and chest space, peacefully lulling you into deep sighs and breathing. Soak it up as you would soak up the sun's rays, lighting every cell of your being as if a gentle hand radiates light on each atom of your being. Bask in the light.

You may see lighter shades of yellows, purples and blues entering your head chakra. Do not stop to think about what each color means as it is not important right now, but just immerse yourself in the actual colours you feel entering your body, forever changing you to the core as they heal you. This energy should make you feel like smiling as a deep calm should set up on your soul. Breathe and stay in this healing energy as long as you can. As many Masters will tell you, breathe in the light, breathe out that which you no longer need. Again, do not stop to analyze the process, but allow this gentle healing to take place. Repeat as often as needed.

Do not feel as though you need to be still for long periods of time with this energy, but know that you can use it to quickly recharge throughout the day. This particular healing will bring much needed peace to your busy days of looking after children and others in your life. Remember that connecting to us above is very easy as you still your mind, and allow the healing energies to enter your body.

Gentle we are.

Gentle we heal.

Forever present, in and around you.

Feel our healing presence as we guide you towards making clear, daily decisions thus creating a solid purpose to your life as we gently move you forward on your individual path.

We truly are there for you, now and forever.

Breathe us in and let go.

Breathe us in and let go, and so we are.

Draw a page of figure eights or Infinity signs to anchor the healing.

Lynn Baribault

Channeled (continued)

Healing is the new energy of forgiveness

In ancient religions, one needed to forgive others as if only others had impacted our lives. Now, the new energy is healing. The word healing not only encompasses healing of others as many of you do, but it also includes healing of self, which is much more profound. When you heal yourself, of course, it is true you can better heal others. But truly, when you heal yourself through the deep and powerful Earth energies, or through the Divine energies of above, you are taking steps towards your own destiny and your own path. For many, this will need to be done through awareness of what your soul's healing needs are during this lifetime and, through the healing Wisdom exercises and prayers of this book which will set you forth in the right direction, as you gain knowledge of your soul's deepest healing needs and desires. The world's energies, from its core to the Light above, are with you in this instance and, trust that your soul is ready for its grand mission here on this beautiful Earth.

Heal often. First yourself, as you are the main caretaker of our youth, then start healing the children and individuals around you. Always heal from the heart, without judgement, fears and/or doubts. By trusting your heart of hearts, you will gently heal others around you, helping set them on their own path, free from any judgment or preconceived notions you may have around what they should do in their lifetime, and how they should go about getting there. That is not your purpose with the children around you. Your sole purpose as a parent, is to be a caring witness to what their life unfolds. Teach your children to trust their instincts, and how to look inside before making a decision by connecting either deep into Mother Earth, or in the Heavens above. Teach yourself first and then teach your children the wisdom of this book as it will forever transform your lives.

Patience remains a virtue, and know that the changes you will feel will not occur overnight. You need to put in the time and effort, but know that as you get proficient in feeling which Healing Energies are needed at a particular moment, your path will unfold more clearly for you.

Be true to yourself, and remain simple in your quest for healing. The support you require is always there for you, through us all who inhabit the energies around you. Connect and welcome us daily in your life. Live your truest life for which your life's purpose will unfold. You, as parents are the anchors in the lives of many around you. Become the Light itself before you share it. Become a Light Healer and you will be a Beacon for all around you, showering Light to those who doubt and suffer.

Each individual, who is in your life, will gather strength as your Light shines even brighter. Have patience and trust in us. We are supporting you, feel us around and within you. Share our Light with your loved ones, and the world energies will be forever changed, ensuring all can follow their true path regardless of the length of their stay here on Earth or the challenges they encounter. Healing is there for all of you. It is powerful. It is true and it is there for all to use. We will never fail you.

From Mother Mary, Divine Light

Prayer from Mother Earth, the Angels and the Divine

Divine Light, I pray to you.
Divine ones, we call upon you.
We call upon your Light of Light to heal us daily, and in our plight here on this Earth.
We welcome your assistance.
We soak in your Light of Light.

We are grateful to you for your access to the Divine Light which envelopes and protects us right here, at this very moment.

We trust the direction we feel our lives should take as we center ourselves on this Light of the Divine.

We accept our sacred path and accept to follow the wisdom you show us here today, right at this very moment.

We still our mind and our heart as we line up our path to this powerful and ever guiding Source of Light.

We trust in you, all Spirits who are our Divine supporters.

We joyfully connect to you daily as we feel our load lightened, our cells transform into beings of Light as we link to your frequencies.

Through your Love, we feel loved.
Through your Light, we feel blessed.

Our path is clear as we trust that we are truly connected to the Divine Source of Light and Healing.

Channeled (continued)

I trust in the Light of Light
I am therefore healed

I trust in the Divine Healing of all Earthly and Heavenly bound Energies.
I am therefore healed

I easily connect to these bountiful Healing Energies in times of need.
I am therefore healed

I trust in its Light as I am guided on my path.
I am therefore healed

I trust the Divine Healing Energies to take me on my rightful path.
I believe I have the strength and Divine support through each and every day of my life so I can be truly present for my children and loved ones.
I trust the Light, therefore I am healed.

I, through the Divine Healing Energies I gather daily at the Source, am a Beacon of Light in my own right, using my positivity to impact others who become aware of my Light.
I trust the Light, therefore I am healed.

I channel Wisdom as I connect to the Divine Source which is there for all of us.

I trust the Divine Light, therefore I am healed.

I trust the Divine Light, therefore I am healed.

I trust the Divine Light, therefore, I am truly healed.

Draw a page of figure eights or Infinity signs to anchor the healing.

Printed in the United States
By Bookmasters